Your Amazing Itty Bitty® Photography Book

15 Key Steps to Learning the Foundation of Photography

This is a 'how to' book for anyone who wants to start taking great pictures, but isn't sure where to start. In this Itty Bitty® book, photographer Mira Zaki teaches you the foundations of photography: Lighting, Color, Composition, and Angles. These foundations combined with her 15 key steps to develop your skills, will give you the tools to start taking professional-level photographs, and creating beautiful and interesting images that get noticed!

Some of the things you will learn are:

- The basic components of photography.
- The most important, and fastest ways to strengthen your skills and take beautiful scroll stopping photos.
- How to start taking professional style photographs.

If you are new to photography and want to learn how to begin to take amazing pictures, pick up a copy of this Itty Bitty® book today!

Your Amazing Itty Bitty® Photography Book

15 Key Steps to Learning the Foundation of Photography

Mira Zaki

Itty Bitty Publishing
311 Main Street, Suite D
El Segundo, CA 90245
(310) 640-8885

ISBN: 978-1-950326-70-9

Dedication Page

Thank you Luminary, New York City for being safely open during the pandemic, and allowing me to sit down and focus on writing this book! I truly couldn't have done it without the peace and comfort you provide in your supportive community and gorgeous space.

Thank you Jessica Joy Reveles for introducing me to the E-Women Network which connected me to Suzy Prudden.

Thank you Suzy Prudden and Itty Bitty Publishing for making me a published author and being the most supportive publishers and humans I could have possibly hoped for.

Thank you to my family for always cheering me on and supporting my love and passion for photography since age 8.

Thank you to The XX, Jon Hopkins, Lindsay Sterling, P!nk, and Pearl Jam for being the soundtrack to this book's creation!

Thank you to my beloved photography instructors who always believed in me and my potential: Anne Sobbota, Chris Broughton, Chuck Place, and the two teachers of my youth who cheered me on from moment one and continue to today: Jeff Smith, and Richele Corbo.

Thank you reader for purchasing my first book- I appreciate you! Now…let's learn some photography!

Stop by our Itty Bitty® website to find
interesting blog entries regarding
photography

www.IttyBittyPublishing.com

Or visit Mira Zaki at

URL www.mirazaki.com

Table of Contents

Introduction

When I was 8 years old, I picked up my parent's Polaroid camera and took a photo. The moment the photo came out, and I shook it to make the image appear, I felt the magic of photography. That moment was the most comfortable I had ever felt, and without realizing it, I found a healing way to express myself. I haven't looked back since! I've spent my entire life studying and immersing myself in photography. In elementary school, I won my very first award (and money which blew my young mind, that I could get paid to do what I love most in the world) for a photo of the Pyramids at sunset in my family's homeland of Egypt.

I have dedicated myself to the mastery of my craft by going to Brooks Institute of Photography and getting a B.A. in Commercial/Advertising Photography.

Three decades later and counting, photography remains my ultimate passion, joy, and a universal language where I can communicate with everyone. It's my great pleasure to share my lifetime of knowledge and experience with you. I hope this book will help you fall in love with the beauty of the world around you and help you capture the precious moments that make our lives extraordinary.

Step 1
The Art of Seeing

If you are a photographer, would like to become a photographer, or simply love photography, you might notice a few things… Lovers of photography are always tuned in to their environment.

1. They have the ability to be observant and see their environment in its true form and essence.
2. They might be the people waking up early on vacation to capture a beautiful sunrise or happily hiking to the top of a mountain to get the glorious bird's eye view of a breathtaking landscape.
3. And…they're onto something!

Photography is the Art of Seeing

1. Mastering the art of seeing makes photography what it is, a beautiful, brilliant moment captured in time.
2. Photography is the world's favorite hobby, and I believe it always will be.

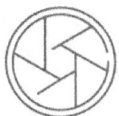

How do you master the Art of Seeing?

- Practice being more observant.
- Stop and look more closely at your environment.
- What is unique or interesting about your environment?

You already have this ability within you

- If you have favorite colors, patterns, or taste in something, you are practicing the Art of Seeing!
- If you love Instagram and Pinterest, you are practicing the Art of Seeing, and may not even know it. You are observing and recognizing things that are pleasing to the eye.

Step 2
Practice, practice, practice

Photography is a skill to master over time, to practice, to play with, and experiment with. Don't forget to have fun and break the rules once in a while!

1. Photography is an experiential art.
2. The more you practice, the more you will develop this skill and tune into your personal style.
3. You will naturally gravitate to photographing something or someone that you find fascinating.

Practicing photography gives you fast, visual proof of what you are doing.

From Polaroids to digital photos, we can instantly see what your photos are telling us.

- Tracking improvement in your photography skills and progress is easily accessible.
- Put your photos side by side when you are practicing taking them. Notice what is different, what has improved, and what areas you might need more instruction or support.

Just like mastering any skill, the more you put into it, the more you will get out of it!

- Practicing taking photographs creates muscle memory.
- Practicing taking photographs helps you develop a style. When you develop a style, you can grow and create a specialty if you choose.

Step 3
Smartphones vs. DSLR

Which camera should you use? Whether it's a smartphone or DSLR (Digital Single Lens Reflex a.k.a big professional cameras with removable lenses), this might not be the answer you're expecting, but... it doesn't matter! When you understand the fundamentals of photography, you can use any device that you want!

1. Mastering the Art of Seeing and the fundamentals of photography will allow you to take a good photograph with any device.
2. Smartphones were designed as light-sensitive devices with wide-angle lenses. This means that they are best suited for natural light during the daytime and wide-open scenes from a distance like a landscape.
3. I encourage you to experiment with different cameras and devices to see which one will meet your needs. The most important part of buying a camera is knowing what you will use it for the most: family vacations, business, to print out photos and hang them on your wall? Think about these before buying.

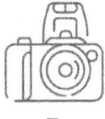

Which smartphone or DSLR should you choose?

Considering the features of the device will be the most helpful guide in making your purchase.

- First, consider if this is for business or personal use.
- Yes, it can be for both!

What will the most important use of your camera be?

- If you want a device or camera for your vacations and travels, look for something that will not be too heavy to carry with you.
- If you want photos of people, animals, or close-up details, look for a camera with the ability to support a macro lens or zoom capability without sacrificing quality.

Step 4
What's Your Story?

Photographs tell the ultimate story, and they remain one of the most powerful ways to tell a story without saying a word. Photographs can be a narrative about you, your life, or a precious moment captured in time. What do you want to share?

1. Think about what you want to share. Taking a photograph captures a moment in time and tells a story.
2. Are you commemorating a special event, celebration, vacation, or a memory?
3. Are you simply capturing the beauty of the world or people that are meaningful in your life?

Photography is storytelling and helps you to form connections through expressions, details, and closeness.

The anatomy of a photograph includes these 4 components that tell a story every single time: Lighting, Color, Angles, and Composition.

- Lighting in photography creates a specific feeling- from the beautiful bright sunlight of the morning to the moody, calm sunset leading into the night.
- Colors have psychology to them, and each color represents specific emotions and feelings.
- The angles of your photograph can tell a story. The closer you are to your subject, the more connected you and your viewer will feel.
- Composition is the way the subject or object is placed in the frame, and it also tells a story. Whether it's a close up of a newborn baby or a wide photograph of a beautiful landscape.

Step 5
Light

Photography means "painting or drawing with light" in Greek. Lighting is the most essential part of photography. Lighting helps you to capture the 3-D world on a 2-dimensional device; a camera, and still experience it as 3-D.

1. One of the most profound abilities you have, is the ability to share your perspective. Photography is all about perception and perspective.
2. The way you share your perspective is through lighting and color.

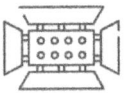

Well-lit photographs are created intentionally, and are put together thoughtfully.

Light has different qualities: soft and harsh. Soft lighting happens around sunset when there are fewer shadows, and harsh lighting appears with the early morning light. Depending on the story you want to tell with your photo, one quality of light will be more appropriate to your photograph's object or subject.

- Lighting creates depth, emotion, and makes a photograph powerful.
- Light communicates in both its presence; reflections, and its lack, shadows.

The ability to understand light, capture it, and control it will give you the skills to take better photographs.

- Your eyes will automatically go to the brightest part of a photograph, and your eyes love the contrast in lighting and colors.
- Sunlight changes quickly and often. Learn to fall in love with lighting and understand it throughout the day.

Step 6
Composition

Composition is the placement of the area of interest in your photograph. Specifically, it is how you "frame" your subject or object, and how you place them in your photograph. Composition is also a way to express your point of view or perspective.

1. Composition is one of the most expressive ways to tell a story in a photograph.
2. A conceptual idea like "love" is often expressed in photographs by being close to the subject, such as a mother holding her baby.

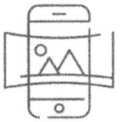

The Rule of Thirds

There are a few rules in photography that are proven to be aesthetically pleasing to the eye. The Rule of Thirds is one of those that states: if a photograph is divided evenly into a grid, resulting in 9 squares, and if you place your subject or object at any one of the intersections of those squares, it will result in a more compelling and interesting photograph.

- Composition is meant to capture the attention of your viewer.
- The key to the Rule of Thirds is to encourage your viewer's eye to move around the photograph and look at all parts of it.

It's ok to break the rules!

- Practice taking photographs both horizontally and vertically of the same subject/object so you can see which composition you like better.
- If your subject or object is not in the perfect center of your photograph, but off-center, it will also result in a more interesting composition
- Composition can be dynamic and attract people to look at your photograph.

Step 7
Angles & Framing

Angles and framing are another way to communicate emotions in photography. There are 6 main angles in photography: Low, Eye-level, Bird's Eye View/Aerial, Worm's Eye View, 45 degrees, and Close up/macro.

1. Angles and framing are best friends in photography.
2. Angles communicate something to your audience. Think of what message you want to share before taking your photograph.

The 6 angles

Each angle has a different result:

- Low Angles are often used in fashion and architectural photography. They give a sense of height and power in fashion and a sense of wide space in architectural photography.
- Eye-level angles are best used for portraits and pets. Being at eye level draws you closer to the person or animal and creates a connection.
- Bird's Eye View or Aerial angles are often used for beautiful landscapes and travel photos. This angle shows both scale (size) and the graphical elements or relationship between objects often used with flat-lay photos or food photography.
- Worm's Eye View angles are used to view a subject or object from below, like the perspective of a worm. This is the opposite of a bird's eye view and can convey strength and power.
- 45-degree angles are often used for food or products. These are the photos that make you feel like you can "reach out and grab" what is in the photo.
- Close up/Macro angles always communicate emotion and details. For example, a close up of a puppy will make you feel connected and like you want to instantly adopt a puppy or hug your own!

Step 8
Color

Light is what allows us to see colors. Color has an entire psychology and study to it; it is another essential component of photography; even in black and white photography there are varying tones of black, white, and gray. Light and color combined create patterns, depth, and adds a dynamic element to your photographs while enhancing the emotional story.

1. Color is emotional and tells a story in and of itself.
2. A basic color wheel includes primary colors: red, blue, yellow, and secondary colors: orange, green, and purple.

Colors have temperatures

Colors can be warm and cold, and using opposite or "complementary" colors creates a very pleasing effect.

- Every color has a temperature. Warm colors are: red, orange, and yellow. Cool colors are: blue, green, and purple.
- Complementary colors create contrast, which your eyes love to look at. Complementary colors are red and green, yellow and blue, and purple and orange.

Step 9
Focus & Zoom

Focus and zoom share a specific perspective. They clearly tell your viewer where to look. If your photograph is of a person or animal, the best place to focus is on their eyes; indeed the windows to the soul.

1. Focusing on the front (foreground) of your photograph helps highlight something specific.
2. Focusing on the back (background) of your photograph is often used to share humor or something odd in a photograph. This technique is often used in advertising photography to share a specific point of view.

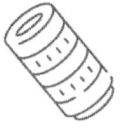

How and when to use zoom

If you're using a smartphone and zoom in, the quality of the photograph is always affected and will have pixelation or blur of your subject/object.

- To avoid poor quality, pixelation, and blur move closer to your subject or object if possible.
- A macro or zoom lens attachment will greatly help with the quality of the photograph.
- If you're using a camera, zoom in for situations that will bring you closer to the subject/object without physically moving.

Step 10
Flash

Flash is an additional light source that is artificial, and can help with low-light situations or to help illuminate your subject/object even in broad daylight. A flash can be helpful with shadows around faces and eyes. For example, a photo of a person on a bright sunny beach during the daytime will often have shadows around their eyes. A flash helps to reduce those shadows.

1. Most modern cameras and smartphones have flashes built-in and are automatically set up to fire during low-light situations.
2. Digital cameras and smartphones are light-sensitive devices just like film itself and are best suited to use with natural light. Balancing natural and artificial light can sometimes be a benefit.

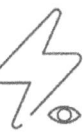

19

More ways to use your flash

It may seem counterintuitive, but flash is often best used during the daytime to balance natural lighting.

- Using a flash during the daytime can help brighten skin tones.
- Using the flash on your camera can help light your scene more evenly by filling in the shadows or dark parts.

Step 11
Filters

The most beautiful filter in the world is the sun! You can enjoy experimenting with the existing filters on your smartphone. The principles of color apply to some built-in filters on iPhones where the filters are labeled as "warm" and "cool".

1. Filters can make subtle changes like softening skin, or major changes to a photograph by completely altering the mood and vibe.
2. Filters can also be used to enhance or brighten colors, change your photo from color to black and white, or add different tones.

Use filters sparingly

Learning to use the sun and natural lighting far surpasses the effect of filters.

- While filters can be fun and creative to use, they can detract from learning and understanding how to use the natural elements of what makes a photograph appealing.

- Using filters to understand contrast and tones can be helpful.
- Experiment more with the sun and lighting rather than relying on filters.

Step 12
Portraits

Photographing people (portraits) is a true art form, and skill to continue to practice. Portraits are one of the most memorable and engaging ways to interact with photography, from magazine covers to family portraits. We remember these photographs for decades or a lifetime, and some portraits become iconic and historically relevant.

1. The same principles apply to photographing people: lighting, color, composition, and angles with the included component of people being animated.
2. Expressions are the most common way to communicate in portraits.

People look glorious with natural lighting

Natural lighting enhances and highlights the features of a person beautifully. Remember that close up angles communicate emotions and show details. Focus on the person's eyes for a compelling portrait.

- Focusing on a person's eyes is the key to establishing a connection in a portrait.
- Using the "Portrait" mode on a smartphone can be a pleasing setting for a photo of a person because it blurs the background.

A Word on Selfies

- If you're using a front-facing camera for a selfie, you will appear backwards in your photo. If you want to take a selfie without appearing backwards, use the timer on your smartphone to take a photo facing forward.
- The best angle for a selfie is at your eye level and slightly away from your face.

Step 13
Pets

Photographing your pets is one of the most delightful ways to connect, and sharing those photos is one of the top three proven photos to stop a scroll online every time!

1. The 3 most important parts of photographing your pet are: to be patient, take a lot of photos as often as you can in succession, and have *a lot* of treats!
2. Pets are prone to move around frequently, blink, yawn, and they may not like being photographed. Having a tripod can be helpful when taking photographs of your pet.

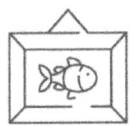

More about photographing your precious fur-babies

Pets are not just a pet, but an important part of your family, work, therapeutic aids, and life truly wouldn't be the same without them. Capturing them in their natural element shares the unique and entertaining personalities of pets.

- Natural lighting without a camera flash is best for photographing your pet. This way, you won't get the green reflection in their eyes.
- Getting down on your pet's eye level will always evoke curiosity from them. Be prepared for a lot of love and affection, and be patient when taking their photographs. It will be fruitful if you are patient and have a lot of treats!

Step 14
Putting it All Together

I hope you've enjoyed learning about photography and that you'll continue to experiment and fall in love with it every day!

1. Remember the four main parts of photography like the four wheels of a car: Lighting, Color, Composition, and Angles.
2. Natural Lighting and the sun are the easiest ways to create compelling photographs; they are also the most beautiful ways to illuminate your subject/object.

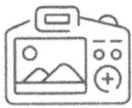

The more you give, the more you get

The more you practice photography, the more you will learn the Art of Seeing.

- Play with colors: primary, secondary, complementary, and different shades of the same color.
- Experiment with different lighting throughout the day: morning, afternoon, and evening.

Don't be afraid to make mistakes!

- Making a lot of mistakes is essential to mastering any skill. Don't be afraid and keep practicing!
- Break the rules from time to time, and most of all, HAVE FUN!

Step 15
Advanced Tips

If you want to take your photography to the next level, here are some advanced tips:

1. Contrast is the holy grail of photography. Contrast shows the difference between the light and the shadows. Successfully doing this creates a more dynamic photograph.
2. Odd vs. Even: Odd numbers of objects or people look more appealing and interesting to the eye. I don't know the exact science behind it, but it is a truth of photography.

More Advanced Tips:

Magic Hour happens twice a day. Golden or Magic Hour actually happens twice a day and shows the most stunning qualities of the sun and natural lighting.

- Golden or Magic Hour does not mean exactly 1 hour of time, but rather the periods of time before sunrise and after sunset.
- This period of time is the most coveted because the contrast is less, and there are no harsh shadows from the sun during these times. This results in breathtaking qualities of light.

You've finished. Before you go…

<u>Tweet/share that you finished this book.</u>

Please star rate this book.

Reviews are solid gold to writers. Please take a few minutes to give us some itty bitty feedback.

ABOUT THE AUTHOR

Hi! Thank you for buying my first book! I'm
Mira Zaki. I am originally from Seattle, and for
the past 14 years, I have made New York City my
home. I am a globally traveling photographer,
photojournalist, instructor, and author. I am the
youngest in my family, and the best dog auntie
you've ever met.

My 8-year-old self who picked up my family's
Polaroid camera never knew what would happen
after that first moment...that photography would
be a great healing, my beloved career, and the
most satisfying form of expression I could have
ever imagined. I am eternally grateful that I was
able to study photography professionally, and that
I get to do what I love most in the world every
day. In 2020, I discovered an even deeper love
for photography by teaching it and creating
online classes!

When I am not behind my camera, you can find
me listening to music (thanks for the healing rock
music and epic life soundtrack, Pearl Jam) trying
a new restaurant... I'm a culinary traveler; I
would and have traveled just for some delectable,
local, seasonal food. You can also find me
stopping every few feet to greet and pet a dog,
reading a book, laughing at a sitcom, or dreaming
about the next story I want to tell with my
camera. I am passionate about social justice, the
environment, and telling the untold stories of the

world. Every day is another opportunity to tell a story with my camera. I hope you will find the pure joy in photography and the possibilities that each new day brings.

If you enjoyed this Itty Bitty® book
you might also like…

- **Your Amazing Itty Bitty® Travel Solo Book** – Marni Allison

- **Your Amazing Itty Bitty® Message Mastery Book** – Sarah Coolidge

- **Your Amazing Itty Bitty® Chocolate Book** – Diana Deene, Deeann Elder and Dr. Carla Rudolph

Or any of the other Amazing Itty Bitty® books available on line at www.ittybittypublishing.com